ENGLISH PHRASAL VERBS
BOOK 2
3 WORDS A DAY

KEITH S. FOLSE

KELLY SIPPELL

WAYZGOOSE PRESS

English Phrasal Verbs Book 2. 3 Words a Day

Keith S. Folse, Ph.D., Kelly Sippell

Copyright © 2024 Keith S. Folse

Published by Wayzgoose Press

Edited by Dorothy Zemach

Cover by GetCovers.com

ISBN: 978-1961953055

CONTENTS

LIST OF VERBS

PHRASAL VERBS IN BOOK 2 (BY LESSON)

Lesson 1: go ahead; look back; stand up

Lesson 2: carry out; go up; take over

Lesson 3: pull out; turn around; wake up

Lesson 4: bring back; hold up; look down

Lesson 5: bring in; look out; take up

Lesson 6: check out; move on; put up

Lesson 7: bring up; look around; put out

Lesson 8: break down; go in; open up

Lesson 9: catch up; get off; put down

Lesson 10: go off; keep up; reach out to

PHRASAL VERBS IN BOOK 2 (ALPHABETICAL)

break down (*first use:* Lesson 8) [*recycled in:* Lesson 9]

bring back (4) [7]

bring in (5) [9]

bring up (7) [9]

carry out (2) [3]

catch up (9)

check out (6) [10]

get off (9)

go ahead (1) [2, 4, 5, 6]

go in (8) [10]

go off (10)

go up (2) [4]

hold up (4) [5, 6]

keep up (with) (10)

look around (7) [8, 10]

look back (1) [2, 5, 6]

look down (4)

look out (for) (5) [8]

move on (6) [9]

open up (8) [10]

pull out (3) [5, 8]

put down (9) [10]

put out (7) [10]

put up (6) [7]

reach out to [10]

stand up (1) [4]

take over (2) [3, 5]

take up (5) [9]

turn around (3) [5]

wake up (3) [6, 7]

INTRODUCTION

Phrasal verbs are one of the most difficult parts of English. They cause headaches for English learners no matter what your first language is. This book will help you with the phrasal verbs that are most frequent in spoken English.

To function well in a new language, you need vocabulary—and lots of it! Some studies say you can do simple things with just 1,000 words, but you can't really speak any language with just 1,000 words. Other experts have said you need 5,000 words, and some recent studies now say you need 10,000 (or even more!) words to speak your new language well. The more vocabulary you have in a new language, the better your speaking and listening will be.

A **phrasal verb** is one type of vocabulary. It consists of a verb and a preposition. The verb is usually a very simple short word like *get, make,* or *take*. The most common prepositions in phrasal verbs (in order of frequency) include *out, in, up, down, on, off, back,* and *over* (Gardner and Davies, 2007).

The problem for English learners is that these two words together have **a new meaning that is not the same as the meaning of just the verb or the meaning of just the preposition**. If you know the meaning of the verb and the meaning of the preposition, it does not mean you know the meaning of the phrasal verb. The meanings are often very different.

For example, let's look at the phrasal verb *call off*. *Call* mostly means to contact someone on the phone, and *off* is the opposite of *on*. But *call off* means *cancel* and has no connection to a phone: *The coach called off the game*. Other examples include *figure out, go on*, and *show up*.

Learning phrasal verbs is very difficult. English has hundreds of phrasal verbs, and each phrasal verb can have several meanings. In fact, frequently used phrasal verbs can have more than five different meanings.

WHY ARE THE 150 PHRASAL VERBS IN THESE BOOKS IMPORTANT?

You can easily find a list of phrasal verbs on the internet, but those are just lists taken from big dictionaries. Many of those phrasal verbs are not so common, which makes them a waste of your time, and your time is important.

In these five books about phrasal verbs, you will practice the 150 most frequently used phrasal verbs in English. This list is the result of an extensive computer analysis of a large collection of approximately 130 million words of spoken English (PHaVE List: Garnier and Schmitt, 2015).

Sometimes one phrasal verb can have five or more meanings, so what should you learn first? You should learn the most common meanings, so the books in this series teach only the top meanings of each phrasal verb based on important information from a very detailed study by Liu and Myers (2020). The meanings are listed **in order of frequency**, so the first meaning is more frequently used than the second meaning, etc. (A few changes from the original list have been made for better learning.)

In sum, these books teach the most common phrasal verbs with the most common meanings in spoken English. Information about the 150 verbs chosen for these books comes from these sources:

Adolphs, Svenja, and Dawn Knight. "Building a spoken corpus." *The Routledge handbook of corpus linguistics* (2010): 38–52.

Davies, Mark. *The corpus of contemporary American English (COCA).* (2008-): available online at https://www.english-corpora.org/coca/.

Gardner, Dee, and Mark Davies. "Pointing out frequent phrasal verbs: A corpus-based analysis." *TESOL Quarterly* 41.2 (2007): 339–359.

Garnier, Mélodie, and Norbert Schmitt. "The PHaVE List: A pedagogical list of phrasal verbs and their most frequent meaning senses." *Language Teaching Research* 19.6 (2015): 645–666.

Garnier, Mélodie, and Norbert Schmitt. "Picking up polysemous phrasal verbs: How many do learners know and what facilitates this knowledge?" *System* 59 (2016): 29–44.

Liu, Dilin. "The most frequently used English phrasal verbs in American and British English: A multicorpus examination." *TESOL Quarterly* 45.4 (2011): 661–688.

Liu, Dilin, and Daniel Myers. "The most-common phrasal verbs with their key meanings for spoken and academic written English: A corpus analysis." *Language Teaching Research* 24.3 (2020): 403–424.

HOW ARE THESE BOOKS ORGANIZED?

There are five books. The phrasal verbs in Book 1 are more common than those in Book 2, etc., so you should start with Book 1 and continue through the books in order: 2, 3, 4, 5. The order is based on an analysis of millions of words of real English.

Each book has 10 lessons. Each lesson has 3 phrasal verbs. That lesson will focus on those 3 phrasal verbs, but it will also review some of the phrasal verbs from earlier lessons, so you should also do the lessons in order.

Each lesson has these **6 practice activities**:

- **Activity 1**: CONVERSATION PRACTICE
- **Activity 2**: LEARNING NEW PHRASAL VERBS
- **Activity 3**: PRACTICING IMPORTANT PHRASES
- **Activity 4**: USING CORRECT PREPOSITIONS
- **Activity 5**: VERBS IN CONTEXT
- **Activity 6**: ONLINE PRACTICE (with a link allowing for 5 different kinds of online practice, including one for instruction)

PRACTICAL ADVICE FOR LEARNING VOCABULARY

You need a lot of vocabulary, and no one can learn this vocabulary for you. A good teacher and a good book can help, but in the end, it's all up to you.

To get more vocabulary, you need to read things in English that interest you. You need to practice speaking in English. You should try to find a conversation partner who can help you practice your lessons of three English phrasal verbs.

Keep a vocabulary notebook, either a traditional paper notebook or an electronic notebook. Every time you see a new English word, write it down. Ask yourself, "Is this word important for me in my English?" If the answer is yes, then ask, "How is this word used?" If the answer is no, then skip it and keep looking for another word.

To remember a new word, look at it carefully. Is there anything different or special about the word that can help you remember it? Is the spelling unusual or new to you? Is the word really long? Does it have any double letters?

Examples:

- VALLEY: You can remember the word *valley* because it begins with the letter V and a valley is shaped like the letter V.
- ENVELOPE: You can remember the word *envelope* because it starts with *e* and ends with *e*, and not many words in English start and end with the letter *e*.
- MUSTARD: A personal example is the word *mustard*. I like mustard a lot, so I know I need that word when

I order a sandwich at a restaurant. If I don't know this word, then I should look for that word in a dictionary and then think of something to help me remember it. To do this well, I am going to imagine a big yellow **M** on top of my sandwich, representing mustard. Whenever you find a new word, try to find something that makes that word different or special to you personally.

- DOZEN: Every time you see a new word that you think is useful for your English purposes, you should stop and make a short example in your head. If the word is *dozen*, then say to yourself, "one dozen eggs, one dozen pencils, one dozen sandwiches." It's okay to practice English with yourself in your own head. This is in fact very good practice. Use the new word and then talk to yourself (silently). It can be something as simple as "I would like some mustard, please." Yes, practice English with yourself by making a short example with each new word.

8 SUGGESTIONS FOR USING THIS BOOK

1. Open the book! Do the lessons! Many students buy a new book but do not complete the book. This book has only 10 lessons, and each lesson is short. Make time to read the book.
2. Do all the exercises. Even if an exercise seems easy, do it. The more times your brain "touches" each phrasal verb, the better your English vocabulary will become.
3. Each lesson teaches you only 3 phrasal verbs, but these verbs can have several meanings. In fact, some have two meanings, but others have five. Everyone

learns differently. Some people can do one lesson in one day, but most people will need a few days with each lesson, so work hard and try to learn these very common, very useful phrasal verbs.

4. When you learn a new phrasal verb, try to learn a very short phrase with the verb. For example, when you learn FIND OUT, you should learn FIND OUT THE ANSWER or FIND OUT HER PHONE NUMBER. When you learn SET UP, you should try to remember SET UP AN APPOINTMENT or SET UP A MEETING.

5. Translations are very good when you first learn a new phrasal verb, but a translation is not your final goal. Your goal is to understand and use the phrasal verb. After you have a clear translation, then make sure you do Step 4: Learn a short phrase with the verb.

6. Every time you see a new phrasal verb, immediately try to make a personal example in your head. For example, when you learn PICK UP, ask yourself, "How can I make an example with PICK UP about my life now?" Maybe you will say, "I need to PICK UP my friend at the airport tonight" or "Please PICK UP the baby." Say this example in your head. Write it down. It is much better if you practice your new phrasal verb in your head before you try to use it in real conversation.

7. Try to use your new vocabulary in your conversations in English. If you have a conversation partner, share your list of 3 phrasal verbs from your lesson and tell your partner that the goal is to use these 3 phrasal verbs as much as possible in your conversation.

8. Do not worry about mistakes. Remember: Practice makes perfect, so practice, practice, practice!

Good luck learning lots of English vocabulary!

Keith S. Folse and Kelly Sippell

LESSON 1
GO AHEAD; LOOK BACK; STAND UP

ACTIVITY 1: CONVERSATION PRACTICE

A news reporter is interviewing the owner of a company.

Read this conversation. Think about the meanings of the **3 bold verbs**. Then answer the comprehension questions.

Linda: Jade, is it okay to **go ahead** and start the interview?

Jade: Yes. I'm ready.

Linda: Jade, what a success story your company is! As you **look back** on your company's history, what are you most proud of?

Jade: I'm proud that our products not only were made to be friendly to the earth but also helped to improve the lives of others. And we made a profit after only a few years!

Linda: That's great. I don't think a lot of companies can say that.

Jade: Well, it wasn't easy. Everyone worked long hours and stayed focused on our mission. Early on, there were questions about whether our product could **stand up to** the more traditional competitors.

Linda: I'm sure that was challenging for you and the others who built this company.

Jade: Yes, and there were many times when I had to be persistent and **stand up for** our values, even when that cost us more money. But the environment is really important to us.

Linda: Did that affect the kinds of workers you hired?

Jade: Yes. Many of the employees we've hired wanted to work here for that reason, especially the younger ones. It's important to them to do work that won't harm the environment.

Linda: So, what's next for you and your company?

Jade: Well, Linda, we're very excited to announce that

we're **going ahead** with our plans to expand our product line for a new target market—teenagers. Based on our research and product testing, we feel this is the right time.

Linda: And when do you expect that to happen?

Jade: That's a great question. We expect the products to be available in about five or six months, but advertising will begin today.

Linda: I look forward to seeing them. Jade, congratulations on these new products, and best of luck to you and your company with that.

Jade: Thanks.

1. What is Linda's job?

   a. a reporter
   b. a travel planner
   c. a director

2. What do we know about the company's financial situation?

   a. The company made a profit after only a few years.
   b. The company has lost money in the last five years.
   c. The company made a profit but expects to lose money with their new products.

3. Why was the environment mentioned?

   a. The company tries hard to have a comfortable working environment.
   b. The company's products do not harm the environment.

c. We don't know from this conversation.

4. Who is the target audience for the company's new line of products?

    a. reporters
    b. women
    c. teenagers

5. What kind of product does Jade's company make?

    a. small electronics
    b. fashion and beauty products
    c. We don't know from this conversation.

6. When will the new products be on sale?

    a. They are already in stores.
    b. They will be ready in about six months.
    c. They are available in five or six states right now, with more coming.

∼

ACTIVITY 2: LEARNING NEW PHRASAL VERBS

Read this information about 3 phrasal verbs. Study the example sentences carefully. To help learn them, read the example sentences aloud or write them on a sheet of paper or in a document.

#31: GO AHEAD (AND)

31: tell a person to proceed with an action

- Even if it rains tomorrow, we are going to **go ahead** with the trip to the beach.
- **Go ahead and** tell us your idea for the birthday party.

#32: LOOK BACK

32: remember and think about something from the past

- When I **look back** at my first job, I realize I made many mistakes.
- **Looking back** at old photographs helps me remember some of the great trips that I took.

#33: STAND UP

33A: rise up from a sitting position or a lying position

- I can't sit at my computer for too long. I need to **stand up** every now and then to stretch my legs.
- When they play the national anthem at a sporting event, everyone **stands up** during the song.

33B: **STAND UP FOR**: show your support of a person or an idea

- You should **stand up for** your friends if they need your help.
- You should always **stand up for** what you believe.

33C: STAND UP AGAINST; STAND UP TO: show your support against a person or an idea

- Teachers, parents, and students need to **stand up against** bullying in our schools.
- I finally **stood up to** my boss and told him I was not going to work extra hours without extra pay.

∾

ACTIVITY 3: PRACTICING IMPORTANT PHRASES

Give the phrasal verb for the meaning. Be sure to use the correct verb tense.

1. get up after a meeting = _____ _____ after a meeting
2. show your support against that idea = _____ _____ _____ that idea
3. remember and think about my time in high school = _____ _____ at my time in high school
4. not sitting on a bus = _____ _____ on a bus
5. don't hesitate to tell us = please _____ _____ _____ tell us

∾

ACTIVITY 4: USING CORRECT PREPOSITIONS

Read the sentences carefully and add the missing prepositions for each phrasal verb.

1. It's important for all of us to be able to **look** _____ at our mistakes and learn from them.
2. I think you should **go** _____ _____ quit your job, and then you can find a better one.
3. If you **stand** _____ _____ what you really believe in, you'll feel better about your decisions.
4. I admire your courage to **stand** _____ _____ your fears.
5. My advice is to **go** _____ _____ apologize. That will help the situation a lot.
6. When a plane lands, you should not **stand** _____ right away. Instead, wait until the plane has arrived at the gate.

~

ACTIVITY 5: VERBS IN CONTEXT

Use the context to select the correct verb for the sentence.

1. I understand why you want to get a new cat. Why don't you just (go ahead, go ahead and, look back, stand up, stand up for) visit the animal shelter on Saturday to look for one?
2. It's important for you to (go ahead, go ahead and, look back, stand up, stand up for) what you truly think is the right thing to do.
3. When I (go ahead, go ahead and, look back, stand up, stand up for) at the first time I traveled internationally, I now realize all the planning mistakes I made.

4. A good manager will always (go ahead, go ahead and, look back, stand up, stand up for) the employees if they are correct.

5. Why don't you sit down? You've been (going ahead, going ahead and, looking back, standing up, standing up for) since you got here.

～

ACTIVITY 6: ONLINE PRACTICE

You can practice the phrasal verbs from this lesson at

https://tinyurl.com/3xv8vbev

Here you can use *Flashcards*, *Learn*, or *Match*. You can also have more guided practice with *Q-Chat*, which offers *Teach me*, *Quiz me*, and *Apply my knowledge*.

Answers for Lesson 1

Activity 1

1. a
2. a
3. b
4. c
5. c
6. b

Activity 3

1. stand up
2. stand up against
3. look back
4. standing up
5. go ahead and

Activity 4

1. back
2. ahead and
3. up for
4. up to
5. ahead and
6. up

Activity 5

1. go ahead and
2. stand up for
3. look back
4. stand up for
5. standing up

LESSON 2

CARRY OUT; GO UP; TAKE OVER

ACTIVITY 1: CONVERSATION PRACTICE

A man is in the garden section of a home improvement store.

Read this conversation. Think about the meanings of the **3 new bold verbs**. Remember the meanings of the <u>underlined verbs</u> from earlier lessons. Then answer the comprehension questions.

Mark: Hello. Can I help you find something?
Randy: Hi. Yes, I'm doing some work in my garden, and I need some help. Some type of plant is **taking over** my vegetable garden. I thought it was a weed, but now I'm not sure. I've got a picture of it on my phone. [*He looks for a photo on his phone.*] Let me <u>look back</u> through all my photos to find it. Okay, here it is.
Mark: Yes, that's definitely a weed.
Randy: Do you know the name of it?
Mark: Yes, it's … um… I'm sorry, I just can't remember the name right now. I think it has a little yellow flower. But this weed can **take over** your whole garden if you don't do something to stop it right away.
Randy: And do you have something here that can do that and keep my vegetables safe?
Mark: Yes, we do. Let's <u>go ahead</u> and look in Aisle 5. There will be a few different products to choose from.
Randy: Do you have one that you recommend for this weed?
Mark: Actually, yes. I recommend Weed-B-Gone.
Randy: That's the best one?
Mark: It is, but the treatment has two parts that you need to do about a week apart. Some people don't want to do that, or they forget, but if you're not going to **carry out** the instructions exactly, then the treatment won't work.
Randy: Well, if it's the best and it's going to save my

vegetable garden, I'll get a bottle of that now. Oh, and while I'm here, I'd like to get a new pair of gloves, too.
Mark: Sure, we sell all kinds of gloves. When you **go up to** the counter to pay, you'll find our gloves just to the left, a little before you get to the counter.
Randy: Thanks. You've really been helpful.

1. How does the customer explain what kind of weed it is?

    a. He draws a picture.
    b. He shows a photograph.
    c. He points to an example on the shelf.

2. Why is this one weed such a big problem for a vegetable garden?

    a. It can take over a vegetable garden.
    b. It has a bad smell.
    c. It has small yellow flowers.

3. If you carry out all the steps with Weed-B-Gone correctly, how long do you wait between steps?

    a. one week
    b. two weeks
    c. five weeks

4. Which statement is true?

    a. The garden gloves are in Aisle 5.
    b. The salesperson says Weed-B-Gone is the best product for this problem.
    c. The customer knows more about this weed than the salesperson.

5. Why did the customer buy new gloves?

    a. He lost his old pair of gloves.
    b. The salesperson recommended using gloves for the weed treatment.
    c. We don't know from this conversation.

6. Which of these happened first?

    a. The customer bought a pair of gloves.
    b. The customer looked for Weed-B-Gone on Aisle 5.
    c. The customer showed a picture on his phone to the salesclerk.

∼

ACTIVITY 2: LEARNING NEW PHRASAL VERBS

Read this information about 3 phrasal verbs. Study the example sentences carefully. To help learn them, read the example sentences aloud or write them on a sheet of paper or in a document.

#34: CARRY OUT

34: complete or make happen some type of activity, such as a plan, an order, an experiment, or a similar action

- My doctor is going to **carry out** a few more tests to see what's going on with my back.
- The new mayor announced a plan to renovate the downtown area, and I hope she **carries out** every part of the plan.

#35: GO UP

35A: rise or increase

- Why does the price of gas always **go up** during the summer months?
- It's hard to believe how much the price of rent has **gone up** in the past five years.

35B: **GO UP TO**: approach or come very near

- I'm shy. When I am in a new place and get lost, I can't **go up to** a stranger to ask for directions.
- After Belinda gave her speech about growing up in a bilingual home, a lot of people **went up to** her to ask her a question.

36: gain control

- If anything happens to the president, the vice president will **take over**.
- My English teacher was sick last week, so a new teacher **took over** our class.

∾

ACTIVITY 3: PRACTICING IMPORTANT PHRASES

Give the phrasal verb for the meaning. Be sure to use the correct verb tense.

1. we did an experiment = we _____ _____ an experiment
2. gain control of a colleague's duties = _____ _____ a colleague's duties
3. smoke rises = smoke _____ _____
4. walk to the spot just in front of an ATM = _____ _____ _____ an ATM
5. the price of milk increased last year = the price of milk _____ _____ last year

∾

ACTIVITY 4: USING CORRECT PREPOSITIONS

Read the sentences carefully and add the missing prepositions for each phrasal verb.

1. Which teacher **took** _____ your Spanish class?
2. In primary school, children learn to **go** _____ _____ the teacher's desk if they have a question or a problem.
3. If a basketball team doesn't **carry** _____ the coach's plan, the team will not win.
4. What should you do if a virus **takes** _____ your computer?
5. Children in first grade can't read much, but their reading rate **goes** _____ pretty quickly over the year.
6. Yesterday, I saw a man I thought I knew, so I **went** _____ _____ him to say hello. I was so embarrassed, though, because I realized I didn't know him.

~

ACTIVITY 5: VERBS IN CONTEXT

Use the context to select the correct verb for the sentence.

1. The student (carried out, took over, went up, went up to) the teacher to ask her a question.
2. The pilot was tired, so the co-pilot (carried out, took over, went up, went up to) the plane for about 40 minutes.
3. Winter is over, so now the temperature will start to (carry out, take over, go up, go up to) every day.

4. Soldiers are trained to (carry out, take over, go up, go up to) instructions.

5. Hey, I have a dentist appointment on Friday. Can you (carry out, take over, go up, go up to) my shift for me, and then I'll work one of your shifts next week?

～

ACTIVITY 6: ONLINE PRACTICE

You can practice the phrasal verbs from this lesson at

https://tinyurl.com/cdknb3x9

Here you can use *Flashcards*, *Learn*, or *Match*. You can also have more guided practice with *Q-Chat*, which offers *Teach me*, *Quiz me*, and *Apply my knowledge*.

Answers for Lesson 2

Activity 1

1. b
2. a
3. b
4. b
5. c
6. c

Activity 3

1. carried out
2. take over
3. goes up
4. go up to
5. went up

Activity 4

1. over
2. up to
3. out
4. over
5. up
6. up to

Activity 5

1. went up to
2. took over
3. go up
4. carry out
5. take over

LESSON 3

PULL OUT; TURN AROUND; WAKE UP

ACTIVITY 1: CONVERSATION PRACTICE

Two co-workers are talking about work.

Read this conversation. Think about the meanings of the **3 new bold verbs**. Remember the meanings of the <u>underlined verbs</u> from earlier lessons. Then answer the comprehension questions.

Sara: Hey there! You're here really early this morning.

Jonah: Yeah, I wanted to get in early today to finish some work before I leave for my vacation tomorrow.

Sara: Yeah, but you're here *really* early! What time did you **wake up** this morning?

Jonah: I **woke up** at 5:00 and decided to get the day started. But I was almost halfway here when I realized I had left my phone at home. So I had to **turn around** and go back to get it.

Sara: Well, even with that extra trip, it's still early. I'm sure you'll be able to get everything done.

Jonah: I hope so. There's a lot of work that needs to be <u>carried out</u> by the rest of the team while I'm away, especially with that big meeting with NeoNexa Labs in three weeks.

Sara: Yes, everyone everyone in the office is certainly prepared to help. We all know how important that meeting is for the company.

Jonah: I'm glad to hear that. I'd really hate for us to have to **pull out of** the competition to get a contract with NeoNexa just because we didn't prepare well enough.

Sara: No, don't worry. Look, Jonah, if I have to cancel all of my weekend plans and <u>take over</u> the project management myself, then that's exactly what I'll do.

Jonah: Wow, well, I hope that isn't necessary.

Sara: Jonah, don't worry. We'll take care of things here, and you go on your vacation.

Jonah: Thank you! My wife and I are really looking forward to these ten days away from the office. She can't wait to be on a beach.

Sara: That sounds wonderful. You're going to have a great time in Aruba, and you'll come back refreshed and ready for the meeting.

1. Which of these statements is true?

   a. Sara starts work at 8:00, but today she is about 30 minutes early.
   b. Jonah is at the office extra early today.
   c. The actual starting time is 8:00, but today both Sara and Jonah are early.

2. What happened when Jonah was driving to work today?

   a. Nothing. It was a normal day.
   b. He saw a really bad traffic accident, which made him late for work.
   c. He had to go back to his house because he forgot something there.

3. What is happening in three weeks?

   a. Jonah will begin his vacation after the meeting with NeoNexa.
   b. Sara and Jonah will have a meeting with NeoNexa.
   c. Jonah and Sara will start working at NeoNexa.

4. What does Sara say about the people in their office?

 a. Everyone is ready to work hard to prepare for the NeoNexa meeting.
 b. She's worried some people don't understand how important this meeting is.
 c. She has to cancel all of her weekend plans to be ready to meet NeoNexa.

5. How long will Jonah be on vacation?

 a. 6 days
 b. 10 days
 c. We don't know from this conversation.

6. Why did Sara mention Aruba?

 a. It's where Jonah is going on his vacation.
 b. It's where Jonah will go for the meeting with NeoNexa.
 c. NeoNexa has their main office there.

~

ACTIVITY 2: LEARNING NEW PHRASAL VERBS

Read this information about 3 phrasal verbs. Study the example sentences carefully. To help learn them, read the example sentences aloud or write them on a sheet of paper or in a document.

#37: PULL OUT

37A: PULL OUT (OF): leave or quit a planned event

- When the 1980 Olympic Games were held in Moscow, more than 60 countries **pulled out**.
- If your leg is hurt, you really should **pull out of** tomorrow's race.

37B: remove something (from a place)

- Sometimes a dentist has to **pull out** a tooth if it can't be saved.
- When we finished dinner, Jeremy **pulled out** his wallet and insisted on paying.

#38: TURN AROUND

38A: turn in the opposite direction

- When we were flying yesterday from New York to Miami, we had to **turn around** because of a problem with the plane.
- Jill, I'm over here. Look here! **Turn around!**

38B: TURN [noun] AROUND: make changes that improve a business or something similar

- I'm voting for Harrison for governor because I think he can **turn** the economy **around**.

- The new principal **turned** the high school **around,** and now it has one of the highest graduation rates in the state.

38C: TURN AROUND AND: unexpectedly do or say something surprising

- I gave Meg a small gift, and she **turned around and** gave me a gigantic hug.
- The new director **turned around and** quit today after being there only three days.

#39: WAKE UP

39: stop sleeping

- What time did you **wake up** this morning?
- Please be quiet or you'll **wake up** the baby.

∽

ACTIVITY 3: PRACTICING IMPORTANT PHRASES

Give the phrasal verb for the meaning. Be sure to use the correct verb tense.

1. open your eyes at 6:00 a.m. = _____ _____ at 6:00 a.m.
2. my GPS told me to go in the opposite direction = my GPS told me to _____ _____
3. not complete a deal = _____ _____ _____ a deal

4. remove too much money from your bank account =
   _____ _____ too much money from your bank account
5. if anyone can change that company and make it
   better = if anyone can _____ that company _____

~

ACTIVITY 4: USING CORRECT PREPOSITIONS

Read the sentences carefully and add the missing prepositions for each phrasal verb.

1. Due to an injury, the runner from Bulgaria had to **pull**
   _____ _____ the race at the last minute.
2. Set your alarm for 5:30. If you don't **wake** _____ early,
   you'll miss the beautiful sunrise.
3. When my niece saw me walk in the door, she came
   up to me and gave me a big hug. She was walking
   back to play with her toys, and then she **turned** _____
   and asked me if I knew today was her birthday.
4. In any big tennis tournament, there are substitute
   players who will are ready to fill in if anyone **pulls**
   _____ _____ the event.
5. I never thought I could pass my math class, but my
   teacher helped me a lot. With her help, I was really
   able to **turn** my grades _____.
6. Joey, **wake** _____. You've overslept again! You're
   going to be late for work.

~

ACTIVITY 5: VERBS IN CONTEXT

Use the context to select the correct verb for the sentence.

1. If I don't set my alarm on my phone, there is no way I can (pull out, turn around, wake up) to get to the airport so early in the morning.
2. During the test, the teacher was checking to see if anyone might (pull out, turn around, wake up) their phone to cheat.
3. Hey, everyone, (pull out, turn around, wake up) so Maria can take a picture of all of us together.
4. I was taking a nap on the sofa but (pulled out, turned around, woke up) when I heard a text come in on my phone.
5. My sister's cat Simon is kind of crazy. Simon was playing with my little sister, and then he (pulled out, turned around, woke up) and started to hiss for no reason.

∾

ACTIVITY 6: ONLINE PRACTICE

You can practice the phrasal verbs from this lesson at

https://tinyurl.com/mrx2tt78

Here you can use *Flashcards*, *Learn*, or *Match*. You can also have more guided practice with *Q-Chat*, which offers *Teach me*, *Quiz me*, and *Apply my knowledge*.

Answers for Lesson 3

Activity 1

1. b
2. c
3. b
4. a
5. b
6. a

Activity 3

1. wake up
2. turn around
3. pull out
4. pull out
5. turn ... around

Activity 4

1. out of
2. up
3. around
4. out of
5. around
6. up

Activity 5

1. wake up
2. pull out
3. turn around
4. woke up
5. turned around

LESSON 4

BRING BACK; HOLD UP; LOOK DOWN

ACTIVITY 1: CONVERSATION PRACTICE

Some passengers are waiting at the boarding gate for their flight, which is 90 minutes late.

Read this conversation. Think about the meanings of the **3 new bold verbs**. Remember the meanings of the <u>underlined verbs</u> from earlier lessons. Then answer the comprehension questions.

Steve: Hey, what do you think is **holding up** the boarding of our plane?

Ted: Who knows? The plane got to our gate more than an hour ago, but there doesn't seem to be anything happening. I haven't seen any flight attendants or pilots get on. No food has been delivered to the plane either.

Steve: Oh, no.

Ted: And I'm **looking down** on the ground and don't see anything happening there either. No luggage is being loaded.

Steve: This is so frustrating! It's **bringing back** bad memories from our trip to Alaska last year. Remember how we sat at our gate for five hours and were never told what was causing the delay?

Ted: I sure do. I hope that isn't going to happen again. The weather here is good, so it can't be that.

Steve: I think I'm going to <u>go up to</u> the counter and try to get some answers. Someone needs to <u>stand up for</u> our rights as passengers.

Ted: Will that do any good?

Steve: I don't know, but if this flight is going to be late departing, then I'm going to ask if they can change us to another flight.

Ted: I'm going to <u>go ahead and</u> get some more snacks for the flight. Once there's one delay at the airport, it just seems like other delays happen, and I don't want to be without food.

Steve: That's a good idea. Will you **bring back** something for me?

Ted: Of course. What would you like?

Steve: Can you **bring** me **back** a turkey sandwich?

Ted: Sure. I'm going to get a coffee, too. Do you want one?

Steve: No, thanks. I have a bottle of water.

Marsha: Hey, I couldn't help overhearing. Do you know what's going on with our flight?

Steve: No, we don't have any idea.

Marsha: I hope it doesn't get canceled. I have to be in Los Angeles tomorrow.

Steve: So far, we haven't had a text from the airline, so that's a good sign.

Marsha: Okay, I guess I'll just keep waiting.

1. What is holding up the boarding of the flight?

  a. No one knows.
  b. The pilot has not arrived yet.
  c. There is bad weather at the destination.

2. Why is the current problem bringing back bad memories for Steve?

  a. He is remembering a similar problem with another flight.
  b. He is remembering standing in line for a long time.
  c. He is remembering the time they overheard a pilot get angry.

3. Who suggests changing to a different flight?

    a. Marsha
    b. Steve
    c. Ted

4. Who is the turkey sandwich for?

    a. Marsha
    b. Steve
    c. Ted

5. What is Marsha most concerned about?

    a. She won't have enough snacks to eat.
    b. There is bad weather in New York now.
    c. The airline might cancel their flight.

6. Which of these statements is true about Marsha?

    a. She is a passenger for the flight.
    b. She is Ted's friend from Alaska.
    c. She wants to stand up for passengers' rights.

~

ACTIVITY 2: LEARNING NEW PHRASAL VERBS

Read this information about 3 phrasal verbs. Study the example sentences carefully. To help learn them, read the example sentences aloud or write them on a sheet of paper or in a document.

#40: BRING BACK

40A: return with something; retrieve something

- When I go to Switzerland next month, I'm going to **bring back** ten boxes of these amazing chocolates.
- The same plane that took me to New York on Monday **brought** me **back** on Wednesday.

40B: cause something like an idea or a memory to return

- Maybe the president's speech can help **bring back** some hope for the people after the flood.
- Visiting my hometown yesterday **brought back** so many memories.

#41: HOLD UP

41A: stay strong during difficult times

- In the interview, they asked me how I **hold up** under stress.
- Maria, I was really sorry to hear about your dad. How are you **holding up**?

41B: raise something with your hands, usually to allow other people to see it

- When a referees **holds up** a red card, the player is taken out of the game.
- In crowded areas, a tour guide **holds up** a flag so everyone can find the guide immediately.

41C: cause someone or something to be late for an appointment or similar

- The current lack of employees may **hold up** the plans to expand the hospital.
- I was **held up** in traffic for more than two hours.

#42: LOOK DOWN

42A: look at something below you

- I **looked down** at my shoes and saw how dirty they were.
- When we **looked down** from top of the mountain, we could see the whole valley below.

42B: LOOK DOWN ON: consider somebody or something to be unimportant or with disrespect

- A snob is someone who **looks down on** other people.
- People who attend this school **look down on** people from any other school.

～

ACTIVITY 3: PRACTICING IMPORTANT PHRASES

Give the phrasal verb for the meaning. Be sure to use the correct verb tense.

1. raise your hand in class = _____ _____ your hand in class
2. cause something like a memory to return = _____ _____ a memory
3. stay strong under pressure = _____ _____ under pressure
4. think you are better than someone else = _____ _____ _____ someone else
5. the traffic caused me to be late = the traffic _____ me _____

~

ACTIVITY 4: USING CORRECT PREPOSITIONS

Read the sentences carefully and add the missing prepositions for each phrasal verb.

1. My favorite part of the game was when the referee **held** _____ the red card right in front Rivera's face and he had to leave the game.
2. Hearing that song always **brings** _____ such good memories.
3. The whole time the teacher was talking to Olivia, she was **looking** _____ at the ground.
4. Our flight was **held** _____ for half an hour by a thunderstorm, so we left Germany late.
5. I don't understand why he seems to **look** _____ _____ your friends.
6. I'm happy to lend you this charger, but when you're finished with it, can you please **bring** it _____? I'm going to need it for my trip next week.

ACTIVITY 5: VERBS IN CONTEXT

Use the context to select the correct verb for the sentence.

1. The teacher (brought back, held up, looked down, looked down on) her book to show us which pages we should open.
2. People from that country often (bring back, hold up, look down, look down on) people from other countries that don't have a good soccer team.
3. Whenever I smell vegetable soup, it always (brings back, holds up, looks down, looks down on) good memories from when my grandmother used to cook it for me.
4. Thanks for talking with me today. I know you need to get home, and I'm sorry if I (brought you back, held you up, looked down, looked down on you) for too long.
5. Wow, you have so much going on now. How are you (bringing back, holding up, looking down, looking down on)?

ACTIVITY 6: ONLINE PRACTICE

You can practice the phrasal verbs from this lesson at

https://tinyurl.com/99sh873w

Here you can use *Flashcards, Learn,* or *Match.* You can also have more guided practice with *Q-Chat,* which offers *Teach me, Quiz me,* and *Apply my knowledge.*

Answers for Lesson 4

Activity 1

1. a
2. a
3. b
4. b
5. c
6. a

Activity 3

1. hold up
2. bring back
3. hold up
4. look down on
5. hold up

Activity 4

1. up
2. back
3. down
4. up
5. down on
6. back

Activity 5

1. held up
2. look down on
3. brings back
4. held you up
5. holding up

LESSON 5

BRING IN; LOOK OUT; TAKE UP

ACTIVITY 1: CONVERSATION PRACTICE

Two women are talking about planning a wedding.

Read this conversation. Think about the meanings of the **3 new bold verbs**. Remember the meanings of the <u>underlined verbs</u> from earlier lessons. Then answer the comprehension questions.

Megan: How are your wedding plans going?

Katie: Mostly good. But doing all these things is really **taking up** a lot of time. It seems like I spend one weekend visiting venues, trying on dresses, and tasting cakes, and then I <u>turn around and</u> have to do it all again the next weekend. It's exhausting!

Megan: Have you thought about **bringing in** a wedding planner? It's their job to **look out for** you and save you time.

Katie: Yes, I've thought about it, but I worry about them completely <u>taking over</u>. It's my wedding, after all.

Megan: I understand, but <u>looking back</u>, I sure wish I had used a wedding planner. My sister just got married a few months ago, and she used a planner. I could give you the name of the person she used, if you'd like.

Katie: Really?

Megan: Yes, she was terrific. Let me tell you what happened. Their caterer <u>pulled out</u> just a few days before the wedding, and this planner was able to **bring in** a replacement on short notice.

Katie: What! No caterer? You must be joking. What a nightmare!

Megan: Right. Could you imagine trying to plan your wedding with no caterer?

Katie: Okay, <u>go ahead and</u> give me her contact infor-mation. I'll think about it.

Megan: I will. Have you found a wedding dress yet?

Katie: Yes! It's beautiful! It's just a little too long for me, so the shop is going to **take** it **up** next week. I'll be very happy to have that done—one less thing that could <u>hold up</u> our plans.

Megan: That's great! I'm sure you'll have a wonderful wedding day!

1. What is one reason Katie is concerned about using a wedding planner?

    a. The planner might choose the wrong caterer.
    b. The planner might not make all the decisions.
    c. The planner might take over the event.

2. Who first suggests a wedding planner?

    a. Megan
    b. Katie
    c. Megan's sister

3. Which of these statements is true?

    a. Megan's wedding planner was excellent.
    b. Megan regrets not using a wedding planner.
    c. Megan doesn't know a good wedding planner.

4. What problem happened with Megan's sister's wedding?

    a. Her wedding dress was too long.
    b. The original caterer canceled.
    c. The planner took over her wedding.

5. What is one thing that Katie is going to do next week?

    a. change the length of her wedding dress
    b. make the final selection of her wedding dress
    c. find a replacement for the seamstress

6. According to the conversation, which of these is NOT part of a wedding planner's job?

    a. to look out for you
    b. to bring in a caterer
    c. to take up a lot of your time

~

ACTIVITY 2: LEARNING NEW PHRASAL VERBS

Read this information about 3 phrasal verbs. Study the example sentences carefully. To help learn them, read the example sentences aloud or write them on a sheet of paper or in a document.

#43: BRING IN

43A: invite or hire someone to come do a specific job or task

- Katrina wants to **bring in** her cousin to help with the planning of the birthday party.
- Our company **brought in** ten translators to translate our catalog into German, Japanese, and Korean.

43B: carry something to a place or situation (that is usually associated with the office or workplace)

- Dan's going to **bring in** some sandwiches and drinks for tomorrow's meeting.
- I **brought in** my laptop because I have the best software for today's presentation.

#44: LOOK OUT

44A: see; view

- When kids travel by plane, they love to **look out** the window.
- When I **looked out** the window in the morning, I saw snow everywhere.

44B: **LOOK OUT FOR**: be extra careful about something that can cause danger or a problem at the moment

- Hey, **look out for** that car! I think the driver is texting.
- Before you sign a contract, you should **look out for** any hidden fees.

44C: LOOK OUT FOR: protect someone else and their needs

- Our boss can be strict, but I think she's **looking out for** us and our future.
- A lifeguard has to constantly **look out for** swimmers who might be in trouble.

#45: TAKE UP

45A: begin a new hobby or activity

- If you have all this free time and are bored, then why don't you **take up** a new hobby?
- When everyone was at home during COVID, people **took up** all kinds of new hobbies.

45B: use a specific amount of time or space for a specific purpose

- The problem with this desk is that it **takes up** too much space in my tiny office.
- Discussing my test results with my doctor yesterday **took up** most of my morning.

45C: collect or take something

- If we order new carpeting from this company, they'll **take up** the old carpeting first for no additional charge.
- At the end of the test, the teacher **took up** all our papers.

45D: shorten an item of clothing, especially pants, a skirt, or a dress

- Can you please **take up** these pants? They're a bit too long for me.
- My aunt **took up** that new skirt I bought because I decided it was a little too long.

45E: discuss a topic or important matter

- Oh, you need to be at tomorrow's meeting because we're going to **take up** the issue of future raises.
- Our teacher said she we will **take up** the topic of the present perfect tense next week.

∼

ACTIVITY 3: PRACTICING IMPORTANT PHRASES

Give the phrasal verb for the meaning. Be sure to use the correct verb tense.

1. use a lot of time = _____ _____ a lot of time
2. be careful with that car on the left = _____ _____ _____ that car on the left
3. discuss a topic = _____ _____ a topic
4. carry something to a place = _____ _____ something
5. begin a new hobby = _____ _____ a new hobby

∼

ACTIVITY 4: USING CORRECT PREPOSITIONS

Read the sentences carefully and add the missing prepositions for each phrasal verb.

1. I remember how bad I was in math in high school, so my parents **brought** _____ a tutor to work with me twice a week after a school.
2. My oldest child always **looks** _____ _____ her siblings.
3. Flying there **takes** _____ almost as much time as driving there because you have to get to the airport extra early and go through the long security lines.
4. It's a really beautiful trip on the train. You can **look** _____ the window and see mountains and trees and sometimes a river.
5. **Look** _____! There's something in the road.
6. If you don't like your new schedule, you really should **take** that _____ with the boss as soon as possible.

~

ACTIVITY 5: VERBS IN CONTEXT

Use the context to select the correct verb for the sentence.

1. I don't like to use the office computers, so I usually (bring in, look out, look out for, take up) my own laptop.

2. Planning a vacation—the flights, the hotels, the tours —always (brings in, looks out, looks out for, takes up) a lot of time.
3. If the pants are too long, you can always take them to the tailor so he can (bring them in, look them out, look out for them, take them up).
4. I love all sports. I've played tennis for the last ten years, but I just (brought in, looked out, looked out for, took up) pickleball about six months ago. I love it!
5. Children have to be trained to (bring in, look out, look out for, take up) cars when they are trying to cross a street.

∼

ACTIVITY 6: ONLINE PRACTICE

You can practice the phrasal verbs from this lesson at

https://tinyurl.com/5ym9mau2

Here you can use *Flashcards*, *Learn*, or *Match*. You can also have more guided practice with *Q-Chat*, which offers *Teach me*, *Quiz me*, and *Apply my knowledge*.

Answers for Lesson 5

Activity 1

1. c
2. a
3. b
4. b
5. a
6. c

Activity 3

1. take up
2. look out for
3. take up
4. bring in
5. take up

Activity 4

1. in
2. out for
3. up
4. out
5. out
6. up

Activity 5

1. bring in
2. takes up
3. take them up
4. took up
5. look out for

LESSON 6

CHECK OUT; MOVE ON; PUT UP

ACTIVITY 1: CONVERSATION PRACTICE

A couple is traveling.

Read this conversation. Think about the meanings of the **3 new bold verbs**. Remember the meanings of the <u>underlined verbs</u> from earlier lessons. Then answer the comprehension questions.

Anita: What do you think we should do now that we <u>woke up</u> so early? Should we try to **check out of** our hotel room early? Or should we just wait until 11:00?

Kevin: I guess we could **check out** early. I mean, there isn't really much for us to do now that it's raining.

Anita: Yeah. I can't think of anything we can do before the 11:00 am check-out time that isn't outside.

Kevin: Well, this weather surprised us all. The forecast didn't mention anything but sun for today. So, it makes sense to catch an earlier ferry off the island and **move on to** our next destination.

Anita: I agree. Let me just **check out** the ferry schedule first.

Kevin: While you do that, I'll <u>go ahead and</u> finish packing.

Anita: So, it looks like we could make the 11:00 ferry if we can leave here in about 20 minutes.

Kevin: Let's do that. I'll be ready in 5 minutes.

Anita: Don't forget to get your umbrella because we'll have to **put up with** the rain on our walk to the ferry.

Kevin: Will do. I'm glad it's only a few blocks away.

Anita: Yeah, if this weather doesn't <u>hold up</u> the ferry, we should be at our new hotel even sooner, and we'll have more time to **check out** all of the restaurants and activities there.

Kevin: Right, and we'll always <u>look back</u> on our stay at this place and remember the great time we had. We really had a good week here, didn't we?

Anita: Yes, it's been great. This room was nicer than I expected, and everyone here has been really nice. The people at the restaurant were especially great. When they found out we were vegan, they pointed out which dishes we could eat. I did not expect that.

Kevin: Yes, you're right. Okay, I'm all packed and ready to **check out.**

Anita: Great. Let's go.

1. What question are the two travelers considering at the beginning of this conversation?

    a. How should they go to the ferry?
    b. What time should they leave the hotel?
    c. How far is the ferry from the hotel?

2. What has been the biggest problem for the two travelers in this conversation?

    a. They couldn't pack all of their things in their bags.
    b. The ferry schedule today was not very convenient.
    c. The weather today was a surprise.

3. What did Anita remind Kevin to get?

    a. an umbrella
    b. a vegan menu
    c. an updated ferry schedule

4. What concerns Anita about the ferry today?

    a. It might be canceled.
    b. It might depart late.
    c. It might not have seats for the two of them.

5. How far is the ferry from the hotel?

    a. about an 11-minute walk
    b. exactly five miles away
    c. only a few blocks away

6. What does Anita think of the hotel where they stayed?

    a. The food and the room were better than expected.
    b. She can't wait to move on to the next place because the room will be better.
    c. She really liked everything except what you have to do when you check out.

∼

ACTIVITY 2: LEARNING NEW PHRASAL VERBS

Read this information about 3 phrasal verbs. Study the example sentences carefully. To help learn them, read the example sentences aloud or write them on a sheet of paper or in a document.

#46: CHECK OUT

46A: look at something to learn about its quality; find out whether something is right for a specific person or situation

- If you want to improve your English grammar fast, **check out** this free website.
- Morgan, do you want to **check out** that new Japanese restaurant with me tonight?

46B: **CHECK OUT (OF)**: pay your bill when you leave a hotel

- I think it's time to pack our bags and then go to the front desk to **check out**.
- Keith, what time did you **check out of** the hotel?

#47: MOVE ON

47A: **MOVE ON TO**: go from doing one thing to doing something new

- After you finish slicing all these onions, then **move on to** peeling the potatoes.
- First, we're going to read pages 50 to 57, and then we're going to **move on to** the workbook exercises.

47B: continue after a difficult situation or event

- I hate working at this company, and I think I should **move on**.
- It was difficult when my dad died, and it took all of us a long time to **move on**.

#48: PUT UP

48A: put something in a place where people can see it

- When you want to have a garage sale, you should **put up** signs in your neighborhood.
- The teacher called on Linda because she **put up** her hand first.

48B: build or construct

- If you're not busy tomorrow, would you help me **put up** some shelves in my office?
- Can you believe they're **putting up** a gas station at the corner of Wilson and Alamo.

48C: PUT UP WITH: tolerate or be okay with

- How can anyone **put up with** that kind of noise all day long?
- She is so rude. How do the people at her office **put up with** her?

∼

ACTIVITY 3: PRACTICING IMPORTANT PHRASES

Give the phrasal verb for the meaning. Be sure to use the correct verb tense.

1. tolerate that noise = _____ _____ _____ that noise

2. continue after a difficult situation = _____ _____ after a difficult situation
3. display a sign to find an apartment = _____ _____ a sign to find an apartment
4. look at a car for sale to see if you want it = _____ _____ a car for sale
5. take a Christmas tree into your house to display it for the holiday season = _____ _____ a Christmas tree

∼

ACTIVITY 4: USING CORRECT PREPOSITIONS

Read the sentences carefully and add the missing prepositions for each phrasal verb.

1. Chopping the onions is going to take up a lot of time, but when you finish the onions, please **move** _____ _____ the potatoes.
2. What time did you **check** _____ _____ your hotel this morning?
3. For most people, it takes a long time to **move** _____ after the loss of a parent.
4. I don't know how you can **put** _____ _____ teaching kindergarteners all day. I don't have the patience that you do.
5. Karina is tired of her long commute to the office, so she said she's going to **check** _____ how much it costs to rent a one-bedroom apartment downtown.
6. Your kittens are cute, but I know you don't want to keep all five of them. If you **put** _____ a sign that

says, "Free Kittens," maybe you'll find someone who wants one of them.

~

ACTIVITY 5: VERBS IN CONTEXT

Use the context to select the correct verb for the sentence.

1. If you're free for lunch today, do you want to (check out, check out of, move on, move on to, put up, put up with) that new Thai restaurant with me?
2. Hey, (check out, check out of, move on, move on to, put up, put up with) this text I just got from my boss. It says someone found my wallet, and they're holding it for me at the main office.
3. Someone (checked out, checked out of, moved on to, put up, put up with) a sign at the supermarket that was advertising a car for sale that might be perfect for you.
4. Yes, it's absolutely true that I have a long commute to the office every day, but I can (check out, check out of, move on, move on to, put up, put up with) it because I get to live in a nice, quiet area that I really like.
5. I'm telling this as your friend. If you hate working at that place, then do yourself a big favor and (check out of, move on to, put up with) another company.

~

ACTIVITY 6: ONLINE PRACTICES

You can practice the phrasal verbs from this lesson at

https://tinyurl.com/4472pr7x

Here you can use *Flashcards, Learn,* or *Match.* You can also have more guided practice with *Q-Chat,* which offers *Teach me, Quiz me,* and *Apply my knowledge.*

Answers for Lesson 6

Activity 1

1. b
2. c
3. a
4. b
5. c
6. a

Activity 3

1. put up with
2. move on
3. put up
4. check out
5. put up

Activity 4

1. on to
2. out of
3. on
4. up with
5. out
6. up

Activity 5

1. check out
2. check out
3. put up
4. put up with
5. move on to

LESSON 7

BRING UP; LOOK AROUND; PUT OUT

ACTIVITY 1: CONVERSATION PRACTICE

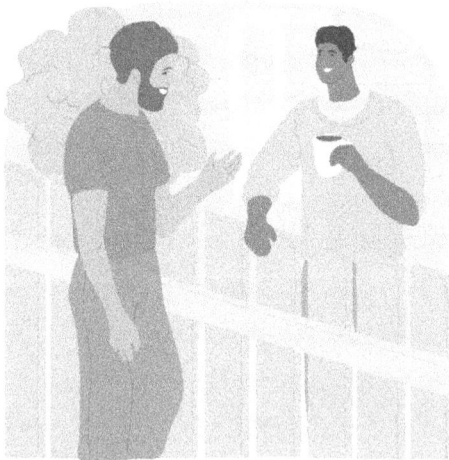

Two neighbors are talking outside their homes.

Read this conversation. Think about the meanings of the **3 new bold verbs**. Remember the meanings of the <u>underlined verbs</u> from earlier lessons. Then answer the comprehension questions.

Chris: Hey, did you see that the new city council member just **put out** a statement about plans for a new park in our neighborhood?

Pat: No, but I'm certainly happy to hear that news.

Chris: We've been waiting a long time for someone to **bring up** this topic.

Pat: Yes, we have.

Chris: Just **look around**. There are so many families with young kids in the area, and yet there's no park anywhere near us.

Pat: Yes, we really do need a park in this neighborhood. Where will it be?

Chris: On that empty lot, with Walnut Street on the front side and Jefferson Street on the back side.

Pat: So that means people can access the park from both streets. Smart.

Chris: It'll be such a great place for the kids to play or for people to spend time together outdoors.

Pat: Any idea how long all of this will take to finish?

Chris: I think about 15 months.

Pat: That seems like a long time. I wonder how soon they can begin work on it.

Chris: Actually, they've already started. I saw them <u>putting up</u> a temporary fence around it a few weeks ago, but I wasn't sure what was going on. I'm happy that it's for the park.

Pat: Well, it's good to hear the city has already started work. I just hope everyone from the neighborhood supports this idea.

Chris: I agree. I guess some people were not **brought up** to love nature, but my parents made sure we experienced being in nature when I was growing up. We camped, and we went on nature hikes. There is nothing like going to sleep under the stars and <u>waking up</u> outdoors.

Pat: I agree. Having a park so close to our home is going to be wonderful. It'll be so beautiful in the fall when the leaves change color.

Chris: Yes. Thanks again for the good news!

1. How did Chris find out about the new park?

   a. from Pat
   b. from a group of neighbors
   c. from an announcement

2. Did Chris and Pat know about this park a month ago?

   a. Chris knew, but Pat did not.
   b. Pat knew, but Chris did not.
   c. Neither Pat nor Chris knew.

3. Where will the new park be?

   a. between Walnut Street and Jefferson Street
   b. only on Walnut Street
   c. only on Jefferson Street

4. When might the park be open to the public?

    a. in only 3 or 4 more weeks
    b. in about 15 months
    c. We don't know from this conversation.

5. Can you go in the empty lot now?

    a. No, because there is a fence around it.
    b. Yes, but only with permission from the city council.
    c. Yes, this area has always been open to the public.

6. What is Pat looking forward to?

    a. walking in the park in the winter
    b. sleeping overnight in the park
    c. seeing the park in the fall

~

ACTIVITY 2: LEARNING NEW PHRASAL VERBS

Read this information about 3 phrasal verbs. Study the example sentences carefully. To help learn them, read the example sentences aloud or write them on a sheet of paper or in a document.

#49: BRING UP

49A: introduce a topic for discussion

- When we meet Mark tomorrow for lunch, don't **bring up** anything about his job, okay?
- I really don't like it when anyone **brings up** politics or religion.

49B: **WAS/WERE BROUGHT UP**: be taken care of as a child from an early age to late teens so you that you learn to think or behave in a certain way

- My sister and I **were brought up** to say "please" and "thank you" for everything.
- I **was brought up** in a home where cell phones were forbidden at the dinner table.

#50: LOOK AROUND

50: go in a place or area to see what is in it; see what is in the area where you are, sometimes for a specific purpose

- We **looked around** for an apartment but didn't find one we liked.
- I **looked around** the house for my car keys but couldn't find them anywhere.

#51: PUT OUT

51A: stop a fire from burning or a light from shining

- What is the best way to **put out** a kitchen fire?
- Please **put out** your cigarettes before coming inside.

51B: WAS/WERE/FEEL/FELT PUT OUT: be bothered or upset by something

- She **was** really **put out** when I asked her not to talk during the movie.
- Some people **feel put out** by the new tax policy.

51C: give information to the public

- The job of a news organization is to **put out** true information to the public.
- How often does any restaurant **put out** a new menu?

◈

ACTIVITY 3: PRACTICING IMPORTANT PHRASES

Give the phrasal verb for the meaning. Be sure to use the correct verb tense.

1. was very upset by what you said = ____ very ____ ____ by what you said
2. stop a cigarette from burning = ____ ____ a cigarette

3. check your room for your cell phone = _____ _____ your room for your cell phone
4. announce some information about the fire = _____ _____ some information about the fire
5. don't introduce that topic at dinner = don't _____ _____ that topic at dinner

~

ACTIVITY 4: USING CORRECT PREPOSITIONS

Read the sentences carefully and add the missing prepositions for each phrasal verb.

1. I **felt put** _____ by what Gary and Hanna said to me. I still can't believe how rude they were to me.
2. When I got to the party, I **looked** _____ to see if I knew anyone there.
3. I would never **bring** _____ that topic at a dinner with people that weren't already good friends.
4. What is the fastest way to **put** _____ a fire on the stove?
5. Just before people leave the plane, the flight attendants usually remind people to **look** _____ where they're sitting to make sure they are not leaving anything on the plane.
6. Lee was born in Mexico, but she **was brought** _____ in the US.

~

ACTIVITY 5: VERBS IN CONTEXT

Use the context to select the correct verb for the sentence.

1. One reason that David became a teacher is that he (was brought up, looked around, put out) to believe that school was essential for success.
2. Victoria, can you (bring up, look around, put out) and see if you can find the button that came off my shirt?
3. Which newspaper (brought up, looked around, put out) the news that the company was going bankrupt?
4. When my dog goes out in the yard in the morning, the first thing she does is to (bring up, look around, put out) to see if any other dogs are also there.
5. I want to know if Melinda has found a new place to live, but I'm kind of afraid to (bring up, look around, put out) anything that might make her feel bad.

∽

ACTIVITY 6: ONLINE PRACTICE

You can practice the phrasal verbs from this lesson at

https://tinyurl.com/548wrdx9

Here you can use *Flashcards*, *Learn*, or *Match*. You can also have more guided practice with *Q-Chat*, which offers *Teach me*, *Quiz me*, and *Apply my knowledge*.

Answers for Lesson 7

Activity 1

1. c
2. c
3. a
4. b
5. a
6. c

Activity 3

1. was put out
2. put out
3. look around
4. put out
5. bring up

Activity 4

1. out
2. around
3. up
4. out
5. around
6. up

Activity 5

1. was brought up
2. look around
3. put out
4. look around
5. bring up

LESSON 8

BREAK DOWN; GO IN; OPEN UP

ACTIVITY 1: CONVERSATION PRACTICE

A tow truck picks up a car.

Read this conversation. Think about the meanings of the **3 new bold verbs**. Remember the meanings of the <u>underlined verbs</u> from earlier lessons. Then answer the comprehension questions.

Michigan Roadside Service (MRS): Michigan Roadside Service. How can I help you?

Zack: Hi. My car just **broke down**, and I'm not sure what to do now.

MRS: We're here to help you. Can you tell me where you are?

Zack: Yes, I'm on Highway 94 just outside of Detroit.

MRS: Can you be more specific?

Zack: Sure. I'm near the exit for South Hill Street.

MRS: Okay, just a minute.

Zack: What happens now? This has never happened to me before.

MRS: I'm going to send a tow truck now. The driver is also a mechanic, so he can tell you what's going on. If he can't solve the problem, then he will tow your car to a repair shop.

Zack: Thanks.

MRS: I'm going to ask you a few questions until the truck gets there. Do you have any idea what's wrong with your car?

Zack: No, not really. I was driving, and then suddenly, the car just lost power.

MRS: Did you hear any noise or anything?

Zack: No, I don't remember hearing anything.

MRS: So, then what did you do?

Zack: I parked on the side of the road, and that's where I am now. I got out and **opened up** the hood and <u>looked around</u>, but I didn't see anything—no smoke or steam or anything like that.

MRS: That's good. Are any lights on the dashboard on?

Zack: None of them now. There were a few lights on inside the car, but I don't remember which ones. I turned the car off, and when I tried to start it again, it was just dead.

MRS: Okay, a truck is on the way and will be there in about ten minutes. I'm going to stay on the phone with you until it gets there.

Zack: Great. Thank you.

MRS: While you wait, please turn on your hazard lights to warn other cars. If you're standing outside of the car, <u>look out for</u> traffic. That's a very busy road.

Zack: Okay.

MRS: Do you keep your owner's manual or guide in your car?

Zack: Yes. Let me **go in** and grab it.

MRS: When you have it, look in the back of the book.

Zack: Okay, I'm <u>pulling</u> it <u>out</u> now. I'm looking at page 157 … Oh, wait. I think the tow truck is <u>pulling up</u> behind me now. Wow, that was fast!

MRS: Great! I'll let you go talk to the mechanic. If you need anything else, please call us back.

Zack: I will. Thank you very much for all your help.

1. Why did Zack make a phone call?

   a. He is lost and needs directions.
   b. His car is not working.
   c. The weather is bad, and he cannot drive well.

2. Where did Zack call from?

    a. somewhere near the city of Detroit
    b. in the city of Detroit
    c. in South Hill City

3. Which of these statements is true?

    a. Zack was driving when the car had a problem.
    b. Zack heard a strange noise from the motor.
    c. Zack saw smoke coming from the engine area.

4. When Zack tried to start the car again, what happened?

    a. Smoke came out of the engine.
    b. There was a loud noise.
    c. The car did not start.

5. Why did the roadside service agent tell Zack to be careful if he got out of his car?

    a. If he turns off the car, it might not start again.
    b. His car is in a place where there are other cars passing by.
    c. The tow truck drive might not be able to find him.

6. What did Zack find out when he read page 157?

    a. The problem that caused the sound from the engine.
    b. The reason the car stopped working.
    c. We don't know from this conversation.

~

ACTIVITY 2: LEARNING NEW PHRASAL VERBS

Read this information about 3 phrasal verbs. Study the example sentences carefully. To help learn them, read the example sentences aloud or write them on a sheet of paper or in a document.

#52: BREAK DOWN

52A: when something stops working

- When the printer in our office **breaks down**, people can't finish their work.
- I'm sorry I'm late. The bus **broke down** on the way here.

52B: BREAK [something] DOWN INTO: divide something into smaller parts to make it easier

- I know this dish may sound complicated to cook, but if you **break** the instructions **down into** just two things—preparing the ingredients and following the cooking instructions—it's actually pretty easy to make.
- Writing an essay is not so hard if you **break** it **down into** planning, outlining, and writing.

52C: become very upset and/or cry because you lost control of your emotions

- Who wouldn't **break down** after hearing that kind of horrible news?
- When the woman found out her dog had died, she **broke down** in tears.

#53: GO IN

53A: arrive at where you work

- I usually get to work around 8:30, but tomorrow I have to **go in** earlier to get ready for the meeting.
- I don't **go in** on Saturday or Sunday.

53B: enter

- It's time for the movie to start. Let's **go in**.
- When the school bell rang, all the students **went in**.

53C: **GO IN/INTO + a place:** enter

- She **went into** the post office to buy stamps.
- Every time I **go into** that store, I spend too much money!

#54: OPEN UP

54A: open something (more informal than just *open*)

- Can we **open up** our presents now?
- I can't **open up** this can of beans.

54B: start or create a situation

- Your diploma will **open up** many job opportunities.
- Learning to speak a new language fluently can **open up** a world of possibilities for you.

54C: start a new business of some kind

- I wish they would **open up** more vegetarian restaurants in this area.
- When is the new airport terminal **opening up**?

54D: talk freely about very personal things

- No one is going to **open up** to someone if they don't feel comfortable with that person.
- I've never **opened up** about all the problems I'm having at work.

∼

ACTIVITY 3: PRACTICING IMPORTANT PHRASES

Give the phrasal verb for the meaning. Be sure to use the correct verb tense.

1. start a new business = _____ _____ a new business
2. my car stopped working = my car _____ _____
3. talk freely about a problem = _____ _____ about a problem

4. she became very upset and cried when her pet died =
   she _____ _____ when her pet died
5. enter the bank = _____ _____ the bank

~

ACTIVITY 4: USING CORRECT PREPOSITIONS

Read the sentences carefully and add the missing prepositions for each phrasal verb.

1. Solving this math problem is not too difficult if you
   break it _____ _____ three smaller steps.
2. Maria **went** _____ the bakery to pick up some bread.
3. I don't know why, but it's hard for me to **open** _____
   to my parents.
4. The movie is about to start. If you have your popcorn,
   let's **go** _____ now.
5. Learning a second language can **open** _____
   opportunities abroad.
6. My car is in the shop again. It's the second time it has
   broken _____ this month.

~

ACTIVITY 5: VERBS IN CONTEXT

Use the context to select the correct verb for the sentence.

1. I don't have to be at the office till 9:00, but I like to
   (break down, break down into, go in, go into, open
   up) earlier.

2. I heard that electric cars (break down, break down into, go in, open up) less often than gas-powered cars.
3. We couldn't believe he was able to (break down, break down into, go in, open up) that bottle with his bare hands.
4. Excuse me, I'm going to (break down, break down into, go in, open up) the kitchen to make some coffee.
5. The plan right now is to (break down, break down into, go in, go into, open up) a new hospital at the beginning of 2029.

~

ACTIVITY 6: ONLINE PRACTICE

You can practice the phrasal verbs from this lesson at

https://tinyurl.com/2xbup9hy

Here you can use *Flashcards*, *Learn*, or *Match*. You can also have more guided practice with *Q-Chat*, which offers *Teach me*, *Quiz me*, and *Apply my knowledge*.

Answers for Lesson 8

Activity 1

1. b
2. a
3. a
4. c
5. b
6. c

Activity 3

1. open up
2. broke down
3. open up
4. broke down
5. go in OR go into

Activity 4

1. down into
2. in OR into
3. up
4. in
5. up
6. down

Activity 5

1. go in
2. break down
3. open up
4. go in OR go into
5. open up

LESSON 9

CATCH UP; GET OFF; PUT DOWN

ACTIVITY 1: CONVERSATION PRACTICE

Two friends are talking on the subway.

Read this conversation. Think about the meanings of the **3 new bold verbs**. Remember the meanings of <u>underlined verbs</u> from earlier lessons. Then answer the comprehension questions.

Zoe: Hi, Stephanie. What a small world!

Stephanie: Yes. I never see anyone I know on the subway! It's good to see you! I just **got off** work and am heading home now.

Zoe: How are things with you?

Stephanie: Pretty good. I really like my new job, and I've met a lot of really cool people there. They even <u>brought in</u> a new assistant for me too.

Zoe: It's nice to hear things are going so well with the new job. It's not the same at work without you.

Stephanie: Yes, well, everything was great until yesterday, when I had to **put** my cat **down.** That was just the worst day ever.

Zoe: Oh, I'm SO sorry. I know first-hand how awful that is. Was he sick?

Stephanie: He was 18, so he was slowing down, of course, but then he just wouldn't eat. When we got to the vet's office, they told us there was cancer everywhere. There was nothing they could do, so….

Zoe: That must have been SO hard.

Stephanie: It was. Well, enough about me. What's going on with you?

Zoe: Well, things with my boyfriend Greg and my parents are good, but my classes this semester have been a challenge. And some of those are required for my degree.

Stephanie: Yuck. Which ones?

Zoe: The chemistry classes. Even though I think I understand the material during the lectures, I haven't done well on the tests.

Stephanie: I hate to <u>bring</u> this <u>up</u>, but have you thought about getting a tutor?

Zoe: No. I keep hoping I'll understand the material if I listen to the lectures again.

Stephanie: Well, if you decide you want to <u>bring in</u> a tutor, I know a good one who could help <u>break down</u> all the material for you.

Zoe: Hmm, I'll think about that. At this point, though, I'm so ready to <u>move on</u> to next semester.

Stephanie: I can understand that. How's your job going?

Zoe: Oh, it'll <u>take up</u> too much time to explain every-thing, and here's where I **get off.** Let's try to meet next week.

Stephanie: Great! I'll text you. I can't wait to **catch up with** you then!

1. Where does the new assistant work?

    a. with Stephanie
    b. with Zoe
    c. with Greg

2. Which of these is true about Stephanie's pet?

    a. Her cat is with Greg.
    b. Her cat has five kittens.
    c. Her cat died.

3. How are things with Zoe's parents?

    a. Her parents have a problem with Greg.
    b. Greg has a problem with her parents
    c. Everything is going well.

4. What does Zoe have a problem with?

    a. some of her classes
    b. some of her friends
    c. some of her bills

5. Who recommends finding a tutor?

    a. Greg
    b. Zoe
    c. Stephanie

6. How do Stephanie and Zoe know each other?

    a. from school
    b. from work
    c. from riding the subway together

~

ACTIVITY 2: LEARNING NEW PHRASAL VERBS

Read this information about 3 phrasal verbs. Study the example sentences carefully. To help learn them, read the example sentences aloud or write them on a sheet of paper or in a document.

#55: CATCH UP

55A: CATCH UP (TO/WITH): get to the place where you should be, especially after falling behind

- I missed three classes, so I have to work hard now to **catch up**.
- She ran extra fast and finally **caught up to** the other runners.

55B: CATCH UP WITH: talk to someone, especially a person you have not seen in some time

- I'm hoping to **catch up with** Helen when we have lunch next week.
- The cousins are planning to **catch up with** each other at the family reunion.

55C: BE/GET CAUGHT UP IN: find yourself in a problem or difficult situation

- At that time, most of my family **was caught up in** the drama of my brother's divorce.
- At my first job, I **got caught up in** some of the office politics, and that affected how long I worked there.

#56: GET OFF

56A: leave your office or job, usually at the end of the day

- What time do you usually **get off** work?
- I go in the office early, so I also **get off** early.

56B: stop talking on the phone or similar device

- Hey, **get off** your phone and help me fold these clothes.
- I just **got off** a video call with my boss.

56C: leave a vehicle (such as a bus, train, or plane) (Remember: GET OUT OF a car / taxi)

- When you **get off** the train, make sure you take your backpack and your jacket.
- Get ready because we're **getting off** the bus at the next stop.

56D: **GET OFF (WITH)**: receive a lighter punishment than you should

- The teacher didn't take off any points for being late? Wow, you **got off** easy!
- How did you **get off with** only a $20 fine?

56E: begin something in a certain way

- My trip to Hawaii **got off** to a bad start when they announced our first flight was delayed.
- Anthony, I'm sorry we **got off** on the wrong foot yesterday. Could we start over again?

#57: PUT DOWN

57A: place something on a surface

- Before we started painting, we **put down** newspaper all over the living room floor.
- She **put down** her backpack on the sofa and then sat down in front of the TV to watch a movie.

57B: write information on a test or some important record

- What did you **put down** for the answer to number 27?
- A diary allows you to **put down** your most important thoughts.

57C: end the life of a sick or old animal, especially a pet

- I can't imagine how difficult it must be to **put down** your own pet.
- Our dog had cancer and was in a lot of pain, so we decided to **put** him **down**.

57D: say something to insult or offend someone

- If you keep **putting** everyone **down**, you won't have any friends.
- He often **puts down** his coworkers when they make a mistake.

~

ACTIVITY 3: PRACTICING IMPORTANT PHRASES

Give the phrasal verb for the meaning. Be sure to use the correct verb tense.

1. Could you stop looking at your cell phone for a minute, please? = Could you _____ _____ your cell phone for a minute, please?
2. Could you stop talking on your cell phone for a minute, please? = Could you _____ _____ your cell phone for a minute, please?
3. reach the same place as the other students = _____ _____ _____ the other students
4. end the life of a sick pet = _____ _____ a sick pet
5. leave work = _____ _____ work

∾

ACTIVITY 4: USING CORRECT PREPOSITIONS

Read the sentences carefully and add the missing prepositions for each phrasal verb.

1. I fell behind in the course and was never able to **catch** _____.
2. When you want to **get** _____ the bus, just push that green button.
3. For now, please **put** those boxes _____ by the door, and I'll move them later.
4. My day **got** _____ to a bad start when thunder woke me up.

5. My mom always says, "Please **put** _____ your phone at the table."
6. I was stopped for speeding, but I **got** _____ _____ a warning.

~

ACTIVITY 5: VERBS IN CONTEXT

Use the context to select the correct verb for the sentence.

1. Can you believe that he (put down, got off, got off with, caught up, caught up with) just a small fine after what he did?
2. I need to (put down, get off, get off with, catch up, catch up with) these groceries before I drop them.
3. The flat tire on my bike meant that I couldn't (put down, get off, get off with, catch up, catch up with) my friends on the way to school.
4. Before the test, we were told to (put down, get off, get off with, catch up, catch up with) our phones.
5. Paul was so happy to (put down, get off, get off with, catch up, catch up with) his college roommates at the reunion.

~

ACTIVITY 6: ONLINE PRACTICE

You can practice the phrasal verbs from this lesson at

https://tinyurl.com/262rc5vb

Here you can use *Flashcards*, *Learn*, or *Match*. You can also have more guided practice with *Q-Chat*, which offers *Teach me*, *Quiz me*, and *Apply my knowledge*.

Answers for Lesson 9

Activity 1

1. a
2. c
3. c
4. a
5. c
6. b

Activity 3

1. put down
2. get off
3. catch up to OR catch up with
4. put down
5. get off

Activity 4

1. up
2. off
3. down
4. off
5. down
6. off with

Activity 5

1. got off with
2. put down
3. catch up with
4. put down OR get off
5. catch up with

LESSON 10

GO OFF; KEEP UP; REACH OUT TO

ACTIVITY 1: CONVERSATION PRACTICE

A nurse and a receptionist are talking at the beginning of the workday.

Read this conversation. Think about the meanings of the **3 new bold verbs**. Remember the meanings of the <u>underlined verbs</u> from earlier lessons. Then answer the comprehension questions.

Receptionist (Alex): Good morning, Caroline.

Nurse (Caroline): Good morning, Alex. Thank you for <u>opening up</u> the office today. How are things going?

Alex: It's been busy! I've had a hard time **keeping up with** all of the people arriving and all of the phone calls and messages.

Caroline: I'm sure you're doing a good job.

Alex: I'm trying. It seems like everyone has a cold or the flu.

Caroline: Well, it is that time of year.

Alex: I don't think we'll be able to see everyone this week. How would you like me to schedule everyone?

Caroline: Well, we can't stay open late to see everyone today, and the doctor won't be available later in the week.

Alex: Oh, I didn't know that. Which day?

Caroline: I think it's Thursday, but it might be Friday.

Alex: I see now that the calendar says he'll be out on Thursday.

Caroline: Okay. One thing you can do is schedule the patients who are here for routine check-ups to meet with me. They might not need to see the doctor.

Alex: I'll do that. And would you like to <u>check out</u> the list of patients who have already called today and then decide which ones should get in this week?

Caroline: Yes. I'll do that, and then the doctor and I

can **reach out to** the patients whose symptoms aren't as bad by phone.

Alex: Okay. Oh, before you **go off** to see your first patient, can I ask you a few questions?

Caroline: Yes, of course. Just let me go into my office and put down my things, and then I'll be right back.

Alex: Okay.

Caroline: Oh, and would you also put out some of that information about staying healthy during the cold and flu season?

Alex: Yes, let me look around for that. I also think we should remind people to get a flu shot.

Caroline: Yes, please do that too. Thanks.

1. What is the problem in the office today?

    a. The doctor is not here today.
    b. Many of the patients came late.
    c. There are a lot of patients.

2. What does Alex say about the phone calls?

    a. People are not returning his calls.
    b. A lot of people are calling.
    c. People are making too many appointments for next week.

3. What is the relationship between Alex and Caroline?

    a. They are coworkers.
    b. They are patients of the same doctor.
    c. One is a doctor and one is a patient.

4. Which day is the doctor NOT available?

    a. Tuesday
    b. Wednesday
    c. Thursday

5. How are they going to contact patients who are not seriously sick?

    a. by email
    b. by phone
    c. We don't know from this conversation.

6. What do they say about a flu shot?

    a. People should get one soon.
    b. It is only useful for sick patients.
    c. People need to get two shots this year.

~

ACTIVITY 2: LEARNING NEW PHRASAL VERBS

Read this information about 3 phrasal verbs. Study the example sentences carefully. To help learn them, read the example sentences aloud or write them on a sheet of paper or in a document.

#58: GO OFF

58A: go somewhere, usually for a specific purpose

- Immediately after Joanna and Ben get married, they are **going off** to Hawaii for their honeymoon.
- I didn't talk to my roommate this morning. I just grabbed my lunch and **went off** to class.

58B: explode (like a bomb) or fire (like a gun)

- When you pick up a gun, be careful or it might **go off**.
- Yesterday a bomb **went off** in the middle of the city.

58C: make a loud noise to indicate a certain amount of time has finished

- Every morning my alarm clock **goes off** at 7 a.m., but I don't get out of bed until 7:30.
- When the oven timer **went off**, we took the bread out and let it cool for 15 minutes.

#59: KEEP UP

59A: continue

- My teacher told me to **keep up** the good work with my English.
- The rain **kept up** for almost two hours.

59B: KEEP UP (WITH): move or make progress at the same speed as someone else

- I like my job, but there's so much do, and it's hard to **keep up**.
- It's hard for us to **keep up with** our teacher because she speaks so fast.

59C: KEEP UP WITH: be aware of the news about a person or event

- Social media lets me **keep up with** my family and friends who don't live near me.
- Sophia likes to **keep up with** the news about her favorite tennis players.

#60: REACH OUT TO

60. communicate with someone in a friendly manner via phone, social media, or in person to offer help or start a conversation

- Whenever one of my friends has a problem, I try to **reach out to** them to see if there is anything I can do to help.
- If you have any problems, just **reach out to** me, and I'll try to help you.

◦∼

ACTIVITY 3: PRACTICING IMPORTANT PHRASES

Give the phrasal verb for the meaning. Be sure to use the correct verb tense.

1. my alarm clock rang = my alarm clock _____ _____
2. continue the good work = _____ _____ the good work
3. communicate with our office = _____ _____ _____ our office
4. follow politics in the news = _____ _____ _____ politics in the news
5. maintain the same speed as the other runners = _____ _____ _____ the other runners

∼

ACTIVITY 4: USING CORRECT PREPOSITIONS

Read the sentences carefully and add the missing prepositions for each phrasal verb.

1. When the timer **went** _____, I took the vegetables out of the oven.
2. It's hard for me to **keep** _____ _____ the other students in my math class.
3. If we have any problems, we're supposed to **reach** _____ _____ the mechanic right away.
4. After college, my best friend **went** _____ on a six-month trip to Europe.
5. I live far from my dad, but we try **keep** _____ _____ each other on social media.

6. I have so many things to do at my new job that it's been hard to **keep** _____.

~

ACTIVITY 5: VERBS IN CONTEXT

Use the context to select the correct verb for the sentence.

1. It's hard to (go off, keep up, keep up with, reach out to) all the new vocabulary in my English class.
2. On the weekend, Kevin and Sue often (go off, keep up, keep up with, reach out to) on their own to hike on Summit Trail.
3. Sometimes I don't hear my alarm when it (goes off, keeps up, keeps up with, reaches out to).
4. When I had a problem with my ticket, I decided to (go off, keep up, keep up with, reach out to) the airline directly to get some help.
5. On my last essay, my teacher wrote, "(Go off, Keep up, Keep up with, Reach out to) the good work!"

~

ACTIVITY 6: ONLINE PRACTICE

You can practice the phrasal verbs from this lesson at

https://tinyurl.com/jjfrpdvs

Here you can use *Flashcards*, *Learn*, or *Match*. You can also have more guided practice with *Q-Chat*, which offers *Teach me*, *Quiz me*, and *Apply my knowledge*.

Answers for Lesson 10

Activity 1

1. c
2. b
3. a
4. c
5. b
6. a

Activity 3

1. went off
2. keep up
3. reach out to
4. keep up with
5. keep up with

Activity 4

1. off
2. up with
3. out to
4. off
5. up with
6. up

Activity 5

1. keep up with
2. goes off
3. goes off
4. reach out to
5. Keep up

ABOUT THE PUBLISHER

Thank you for your time and attention! If you found the book useful, we hope you will leave a short review on the site where you purchased this book to let other readers know of your experience.

To be notified about new titles and special contests, events, and sales from Wayzgoose Press, please visit our website at

http://wayzgoosepress.com

and sign up for our mailing list. (We send email infrequently, and you can unsubscribe at any time.)

∽

www.ingramcontent.com/pod-product-compliance
Lightning Source LLC
Chambersburg PA
CBHW060812050426
42449CB00008B/1640